4 WEEKS TO A NEW FOREVER

Keith Davis
&
Ty Hughey

Keith Davis & Ty Hughey

ISBN:

DEDICATION

This book is dedicated to Terrance Mcbroom. Your presence is felt as if you just left the room. Thank you for your big heart and the countless smiles you've put on everybody's faces.

We miss you! We thank you for watching over us. We love you!!!

This book is dedicated to Anthony J Hughey.

To the greatest man I know. You gave me a strong foundation and belief system. You gave me the proper tools to challenge myself to evolve.

Insight, clarity and growth equals vision.

Never stop learning and build your own table.

TERRANCE
MCBROOM

ANTHONY J.
HUGHEY

Keith Davis & Ty Hughey

CONTENTS

ACKNOWLEDGMENTS

"I MATTER"

"I MATTER"

"I MATTER"

Don't let a day go by without you repeating
this to yourself because:

YOU MATTER!!!

4 WEEKS TO A NEW FOREVER

LET'S GOOO!!

LET'S GOOO!!

LET'S GOOO!!

LET'S GOOO!!

LET'S GOOO BABY!!

These next 4 weeks are going to change your life FOREVER!!

> ➢ Forget what happened to you...

> ➢ Forget what they said you couldn't do...

> ➢ Forget about giving up on yourself...

4 WEEKS TO A NEW FOREVER is a guide to bring you to a whole new level of thinking...

Take ownership and realize "**It's My Fault** that I am where I am..."

No matter what we go through, Tough Times are going to make us, not break us...

Every day we wake up, know that **We Blessed**, and conquer the day, week, month, year, and FOREVER!!!

It's time to take control over your life and live on your terms.....

So, LET'S GOOOOOOOOO!!

DAY 1: My Fault Mondays!!

We can blame everyone else for where we are, for our circumstances, but until we look ourselves in the mirror and say, **"It's My Fault,"** we gonna stay stuck!!

When everything in our lives is crumbling before our eyes, it's easy to point the finger and make excuses. Taking ownership and saying, "It's My Fault," then changing our behavior is how we can change our lives!!

I was wrong!!

I made a bad decision!!

I hit the snooze button!!

I didn't put in the effort!!

I could've done this or that better!!

Get to a point where you can say, "It's My Fault," correct it, and Let's Gooo!!

I KNOW THAT IT'S MY FAULT THAT:

_____

_____

DAY 2: Talk About It Tuesday's!!

➢ Depressed? **Talk About It**!!

➢ Hurt? Talk About It!!

➢ Can't get over the hump? Talk About It!!

➢ Confused? Talk About It!!

Stop letting that pain or whatever you're going through hold you back from living and Talk About It!!

➢ Can't trust nobody?

➢ Think you gonna be judged?

➢ No support system?

Call me, inbox me, contact me so we can Talk About It and get to a solution!!

Don't bottle up your problems because the bottle might slip and break, and the mess might be too big to clean up, so Talk About It and Let's Gooo!!

IN ORDER FOR ME TO MOVE ON IN MY LIFE, I NEED TO TALK ABOUT:

_____

_____

_____

_____

_____

_____

_____

_____

_____

_____

_____

_____

_____

_____

DAY 3: Weak Minded Wednesdays!!

It's easy to be a follower, easy to be manipulated into thinking that we are not enough. We gotta stop being **Weak-Minded**. Be a leader and know that we are Amazing!!

To strengthen a muscle, it has to be exercised; more weight has to be added in order for it to get stronger, so let's get rid of being Weak-Minded by reading, praying, affirmation, forgiveness, and let's strengthen our minds!!

> ➤ I AM Amazing!!
>
> ➤ I WILL NOT surrender to my circumstances!!
>
> ➤ I CAN give and receive love!!
>
> ➤ I BELIEVE IN ME!!

Get out of the habit of being Weak-Minded and Let's Gooo!!

I AM NO LONGER WEAK MINDED!!

I WILL STRENGTHEN MY MIND BY:

_____

_____

_____

_____

_____

_____

_____

_____

_____

_____

_____

_____

_____

_____

DAY 4: Thankful Thursdays!!

I have all my thoughts. I am able to laugh. I can breathe. I am alive. I am **Thankful**!!

What I went through, I grew through. I made it out. I might've gotten scraped, banged up, bruised, but I made it out of that situation, I am

THANKFUL!!

- ➤ I'm Thankful for my family!!
- ➤ I'm thankful for my kids!!
- ➤ I'm Thankful for my past for making me tougher!!
- ➤ I'm Thankful for my goals, dreams, and ambitions that I will achieve by any means necessary!!

WHEN I THINK ABOUT MY LIFE, I AM THANKFUL FOR:

_____

_____

_____

_____

_____

_____

_____

_____

_____

_____

_____

_____

_____

_____

_____

_____

DAY 5: Feed Me Fridays!!

Anybody that knows me, knows that I'm always hungry, but I'm really starving for success, so **Feed Me** knowledge in order for me to give it out so we can all eat together!!

If you got an attitude all the time, always mad, what you're really saying is Feed Me love and affection, but that's what you need to give out in order to receive it!!

We gotta stop hating, stop with these false perceptions of hearing what we want to hear, communicate effectively, **FEED** each other strategies to better our lives, Feed each other love to dissipate the hate, Feed each other wisdom to gain wealth and Let's Gooo Baby!!

THE MOST IMPORTANT THINGS THAT I AM MISSING IN MY LIFE AND I WANT SOMEONE TO FEED ME IS:

_____

_____

_____

_____

Keith Davis & Ty Hughey

_____

_____

_____

_____

_____

_____

_____

_____

_____

_____

_____

DAY 6: Save It Saturdays!!

When pain and trauma happens in our lives, we can instantly save those memories and revert to them and let them trouble us...Remember when you were a blessing to someone?! Remember when you felt better than you've ever felt?! Remember when you reached that goal?! Capture those moments, Save It, and revert to those whenever you need to in order to push through!!

Say no to buying unnecessary things. Take that money and **Save It** and over time you can start that business, have the down payment for that house, go on that trip!!

Save It!!! Each other, let's stop judging one another, stop playing people, lift each other up, compliment, smile, speak first!!

Let's Gooo!!

I CAN GET FURTHER IF I PUT THE FOLLOWING THINGS IN MY LIFE SAVINGS ACCOUNT (This doesn't mean just money):

_____

_____

_____

_____

_____

_____

_____

_____

_____

_____

_____

_____

_____

_____

Day 7: Stop Sleeping Sundays!!

We have the ability to be, do, and have anything we want in life if we **Stop Sleeping**!!

Sometimes, we let opportunities slip through our fingers because we hitting the snooze button on ourselves. We gotta Stop Sleeping and **Wake Up**!!

I wake up some days and look at the clock like, just 5 or 10 more minutes, which turns into an hour and then I'm late, and depending on what I'm late for, it could ruin everything I've worked for, so we gotta STOP SLEEPING, get up, and go get it!!

Let's Gooo!!

IF ONLY I WOULD STOP SLEEPING ON THESE THINGS, I CAN ACCOMPLISH:

_____

_____

_____

_____

_____

_____

_____

_____

_____

_____

_____

_____

_____

_____

_____

_____

Week One Reflections

WEEKLY REFLECTION AND CORRECTION

- WHAT DID YOU LEARN FROM YOUR FAILURES?

_____

_____

_____

_____

_____

_____

_____

_____

_____

- ## WHAT DID YOU LEARN FROM YOUR SUCCESSES?

_____

_____

_____

_____

_____

_____

_____

_____

_____

_____

_____

- HOW DO YOU FEEL ABOUT YOUR OBSERVATIONS?

_____

_____

_____

_____

_____

_____

_____

_____

_____

_____

_____

_____

DAY 8: Make A Change Mondays!!

When you've had enough, when you're tired, when your situation becomes unbearable, take the necessary steps to **Make A Change**!!

Sometimes, it took me three, four, even five times to realize what I was doing was wrong, INSANITY, and I decided to Make A Change!!

Nothing in our lives will be different until we Make A Change to our mindsets and discipline ourselves!!

So, Make A Change today and Let's Gooo!!

I KNOW I NEED TO MAKE A CHANGE IN THESE AREAS OF MY LIFE:

_____

_____

_____

_____

_____

_____

_____

_____

_____

_____

_____

_____

_____

_____

_____

_____

_____

_____

_____

_____

DAY 9: Tough Times Tuesdays!!

We can scream, cry, kick, punch the air, ask others for help, do whatever it is we gotta do EXCEPT give up, to get through **Tough Times**!!

Everybody at some point in their lives experiences Tough Times, but the more we tell ourselves, "Nothing can stop me, nothing can break me," the easier it is for us to push through!!

I know that situation you're in may seem like the end of the world, but when you persevere and push through these Tough Times, it will be the beginning of a new mindset, new confidence, new you!!

➤ Keep going!!

➤ Keep pushing!!

➤ Keep grinding!!

➤ Keep beating the odds and LET'S GOOO!!

I BELIEVE IN MYSELF SO MUCH THAT I KNOW TOUGH TIMES WILL NOT BREAK ME BECAUSE:

_____

_____

_____

_____

_____

_____

_____

_____

_____

_____

_____

_____

_____

DAY 10: We Litt Wednesdays!!

We need to get to a point where **We Litt** is not only in the club, bars, drinking, and smoking!!

We need to take care of our responsibilities and say "We Litt" with our families!!

Get disciplined with our spending habits and let our bank statements announce that We Litt!!

Take the necessary steps to further our careers, our businesses and let our work ethic say, "We Litt!!"

Teach our children the things and values that are necessary to survive in this day and age so they can say, "We Litt!!"

Dig deep and get through any struggles, problems, or situations you or your loved ones are going through so y'all lives will be Litt!!

- ➢ You are AMAZING!!
- ➢ Nothing Can Stop You!!
- ➢ We Litt!!
- ➢ Let's Gooo!!

THESE ARE THE AREAS THAT I WANT TO BE LITT:

_____

DAY 11: Thriving Thursdays!!

Getting knocked down hurts, but staying down is more painful, get up and start **Thriving**!!

When we use that anger as fuel, when we turn that pain into motivation, we begin Thriving on a level we never imagined!!

Despite the No's, go until you get a Yes. Keep Thriving!!

Save until you get to that goal. Keep Thriving!!

So what they left you! They are missing out on someone amazing. Keep Thriving!!

I know it's hard. I know you want to give up, but you are almost there. Keep Thriving!!

Let's Gooo!!

I AM AND I WILL BE THRIVING IN MY LIFE BY DOING:

_____

_____

_____

_____

_____

_____

_____

_____

_____

_____

_____

_____

_____

_____

_____

_____

_____

_____

DAY 12: Fly Swatting Fridays!!

To catch a fly, to reach our goals, we must have patience. We must study what we want, and we must attack it!!

While chasing our goals, we are gonna run into obstacles. We gonna hit our knee on the table while chasing the fly, but we gotta keep going after it, keep pursuing our dreams, and never give up!!

- ➤ **Catch that fly**!!
- ➤ Reach the goal!!
- ➤ Get to the spot!!
- ➤ Give it everything you got despite your circumstances!!

Let's Gooo!!!!

THIS IS THE 'FLY' IN MY LIFE THAT I AM GOING TO SWATT:

_____

_____

_____

_____

_____

_____

_____

_____

_____

_____

_____

_____

_____

_____

_____

Day 13: Size It Up Saturdays!!

We gotta stop running from our problems. **Size It Up**, and beat whatever we going through!!

It's ok to be afraid; it's ok to have doubts; it's ok to be unsure, but Size It Up, look fear, doubt, and unsureness in the face and say Let's Gooo, you will not beat me!!

You can get through anything in life if you Size It Up and take it head on!!

Of course, we gonna get knocked down. Of course, we gonna fall, but when we get off the floor, Size It Up, and swing back, we start to win!!!

Let's Gooo!!

I KNOW I HAVE BEEN RUNNING, BUT THIS IS THE THING/S THAT I NEED TO SIZE UP AND BEAT:

_____

_____

_____

_____

_____

_____

_____

_____

_____

_____

_____

_____

_____

_____

_____

_____

_____

DAY 14: Self Sundays!!

Before you make sure everyone else is good, before you use all of your energy to help others, first take care of your**Self**!!

> ➤ Self esteem!!

> ➤ Self confidence!!

> ➤ Self motivation!!

> ➤ Self defense!!

> ➤ Self worth!!

> ➤ Self love!!

You control your thoughts; you control your mind; you control your emotions; you control your actions; you control your life; you control yourSelf!!

You are amazing, you are a Queen/King. Nothing can stop you. Keep going and do what's right for YOU!!

Let's Gooo!!

FROM NOW ON I AM GOING TO TAKE CARE OF MYSELF BY:

_____

_____

_____

_____

_____

_____

_____

_____

_____

_____

_____

_____

_____

_____

Week Two Reflections

WEEKLY REFLECTION AND CORRECTION

- WHAT DID YOU LEARN FROM YOUR FAILURES?

_____

_____

_____

_____

_____

_____

_____

_____

_____

- ## WHAT DID YOU LEARN FROM YOUR SUCCESSES?

_____

_____

_____

_____

_____

_____

_____

_____

_____

_____

_____

- # HOW DO YOU FEEL ABOUT YOUR OBSERVATIONS?

_____

_____

_____

_____

_____

_____

_____

_____

_____

_____

DAY 15: Mustard Seed Mondays!!

All it takes is for you to believe, to have the faith of a **Mustard Seed**, and you can be, do and have ANYTHING!!

You will get through it; this thing will not break you. You are worth it; just have Mustard Seed faith to see your way through whatever you're battling!!

> ➢ Hope
> ➢ Belief
> ➢ Courage
> ➢ Confidence
> ➢ Will

Faith, the size of a Mustard Seed, is all you need to get there!!

Let's Gooo!!

BY HAVING THE FAITH OF A MUSTARD SEED, THE FOLLOWING THINGS CAN OCCUR IN MY LIFE:

_____

_____

_____

_____

_____

_____

_____

_____

_____

_____

_____

_____

_____

_____

DAY 16: Take A Loss Tuesdays!!

In my experience, I had to **Take A Loss**, sometimes the same loss multiple times, in order to learn and grow from it!!

What we can't do when we Take A Loss: revel in it. We can't feel sorry for ourselves. We have to take responsibility, make the necessary adjustments, and keep going!!

Nobody likes losing, NOBODY, so when we Take A Loss, we gotta turn it into a victory by any means!!

> ➤ You are Worth It!!
> ➤ You are Amazing!!
> ➤ Believe in YOURSELF!!

Let's Gooo!!

THESE ARE THE LOSSES I HAVE TAKEN AND THIS IS HOW I HAVE/WILL TURN THEM INTO A VICTORY:

_____

_____

_____

Keith Davis & Ty Hughey

40

DAY 17: We Blessed Wednesdays!!

For me to write this book and for you to be able to read it, **We Blessed**!!

Focusing on what we don't have, paying attention to what we lack in material objects, concentrating on being broke, is taking away from us realizing that We Blessed, and every day is a chance to better ourselves and our situations!!

Get up and take the deepest breath you ever took. You are alive. We Blessed!!

Whatever you are going through, there's a lesson in it. You are gonna grow because of it. Realize that We Blessed and get through it!!

Let's Gooo!!

THIS IS EVERY REASON THAT I AM BLESSED:

_____

_____

_____

_____

DAY 18: That Ain't Me Thursdays!!

When you are not putting your best foot forward, when you are feeling sorry for yourself, when you want to give up on yourself, remember who you are, tell yourself, **"That Ain't Me,"** and get it together!!

Stop following the crowd. Stop going with the latest trends because everybody else doing it. Stop being a clone. Realize That Ain't Me and be the leader you were always meant to be!!

Listen, I know it's easy to get persuaded; peer pressure can be difficult, but don't do what you know is wrong. Don't do what you know can lead to your demise. Repeatedly say "That Ain't Me." Do what's right and Let's Gooo!!

I KNOW WHEN I AM NOT MYSELF AND THIS IS WHAT I AM GOING TO DO IN A SITUATION WHEN I KNOW THIS AIN'T ME:

_____

_____

_____

DAY 19: Forever Fridays!!

WE DO NOT HAVE FOREVER!!

Do the most with your TODAY because tomorrow is not promised, and **Forever** is nonexistent!!

I'll do it tomorrow, which turns into next week, which turns into next month, which turns into next year, which turns into never. **WE DO NOT HAVE FOREVER!!**

There are people who didn't wake up today that thought they had Forever to reach their goals, thought that they had more time to say, "I love you," that would give anything to have one more second, minute, hour, day......Stop Playing with life and LET'S GOOO!!

I DO NOT HAVE FOREVER, SO I WILL TAKE ACTION TODAY BY DOING:

_____

_____

_____

_____

_____

_____

_____

_____

_____

_____

_____

_____

_____

_____

_____

_____

_____

DAY 20: Same Lies Saturdays

You're not tired of saying, 'I'm getting up earlier', 'I'm saving money this week', I'm filling out those applications today', and not doing those things?! Stop telling yourself those **Same Lies** and do what you say you gonna do!!

➢ I can't...

➢ I'm not worth it...

➢ I'm not smart enough...

➢ I will never accomplish that...

These are the Same Lies that hold us back from reaching our goals.

Stop lying to yourself; know that you are AMAZING and Let's Gooo!!

I WILL NO LONGER TELL MYSELF THESE SAME LIES:

_____

_____

_____

_____

Keith Davis & Ty Hughey

_____

_____

_____

_____

_____

_____

_____

_____

_____

_____

_____

_____

_____

DAY 21: Stop Settling Sundays!!

Stop Settling for that job you hate and go after that career you've dreamed of!!

> ➤ Stop Settling for mediocrity!!

> ➤ Stop Settling for those relationships that only bring you down!!

> ➤ Stop Settling and go after that thing you've always wanted!!

We gotta Stop Settling for the things that are holding us back from excelling in our lives!!

C'mon, Get to It! Stop Settling!!

Let's Gooo!!

I WILL STOP SETTLING FOR LESS THAN I DESERVE AND GO AFTER THESE THINGS:

_____

_____

_____

_____

_____

_____

_____

_____

_____

_____

_____

_____

_____

_____

_____

_____

_____

Week Three Reflections

WEEKLY REFLECTION AND CORRECTION:

- WHAT DID YOU LEARN FROM YOUR FAILURES?

_____

_____

_____

_____

_____

_____

_____

- WHAT DID YOU LEARN FROM YOUR SUCCESSES?

_____

Keith Davis & Ty Hughey

_____

_____

_____

_____

_____

_____

- HOW DO YOU FEEL ABOUT YOUR OBSERVATIONS?

_____

_____

_____

_____

_____

_____

DAY 22: Man Up Mondays!!

We either heading into a storm, in the midst of a storm, or coming outta one, so we gotta **Man Up**, get through it, and get to the sunshine!!

Some of us can only see dark clouds, hear thunder, see lightning, and feel the rain, but we cannot afford to get swept up in the storm. We must Man Up, keep pushing through, and make it out!!

I know it's one thing after another. I know it's hard. I know it's lonely. I know you feel like giving up, but Man Up. You will get through this. You will come out a winner. You will succeed!!

Let's Gooo!!

I NEED TO MAN UP AND:

_____

_____

_____

_____

_____

_____

_____

_____

_____

_____

_____

_____

_____

_____

_____

_____

DAY 23: Take It On Tuesday!!

We are done running from our problems, finished running from our destiny because of a little adversity. We gotta **Take It On** and live the life we are meant to!!

In order for us to grow, we must face our fears, realize our weaknesses, and look at our problems in the face, and Take It On !!

Every struggle we face, every adversity we encounter, every battle we show up for, if we learn how to Take It On. NOTHING will be able to stop us!!

Let's Gooo!!

NOTHING WILL STOP ME BY MY ABILITY TO TAKE ON:

_____

_____

_____

_____

_____

DAY 24: Workout Wednesdays!!

When you are feeling sluggish, unmotivated, not yourself, **Workout**! Get moving and watch the transformation in you!!

We gotta be hungry for growth, seek knowledge, read, be around those that are smarter, so we can Workout our minds!!

Pray, fast, read scriptures, go to church, do whatever it takes to have a relationship with your higher power so you can Workout your spirit. Be at peace and push through anything!!

Let's Gooo!!

I WILL TAKE CARE OF MY MIND, BODY, and SOUL BY WORKING OUT:

_____

_____

_____

_____

_____

Keith Davis & Ty Hughey

_____

_____

_____

_____

_____

_____

_____

_____

_____

_____

_____

_____

DAY 25: Think It, Then Do It Thursdays!!

How many ideas come across our minds that we never act upon, then we see exactly what we thought done by someone else? So, it's urgent that we **Think It, Then Do It**!!

We think we need all the answers before we get started on something, and soon we lose that fire and never get it going, looking back wondering if that was the life changing thing we missed out on. But if we Think It, Then Do it, there is no telling where we can go, what we can be, or whose lives we can change!!

- ➢ Visualize-Write it — Execute
- ➢ Visualize-Write it — Execute
- ➢ Visualize-Write it — Execute

Think It, Then Do It and Let's Gooo!!

I AM THINKING THEN DOING:

_____

_____

_____

_____

DAY 26: Fast Forward Fridays!!

Visualize it, see it, feel it, and **Fast Forward** yourself to where you want to be, then work towards it, every single day!!

We gotta stop rewinding our lives to our past failures, to our bad decisions, to those relationships that weren't good for us, and Fast Forward to the love we know we deserve. Fast Forward to us in the careers we've always wanted. Fast Forward to the life we've always imagined and get there!!!

Let's Gooo!!

WHEN I FAST FORWARD MY LIFE, I SEE MYSELF:

_____

_____

_____

_____

_____

_____

_____

_____

_____

_____

_____

_____

_____

_____

_____

_____

_____

_____

Day 27: Start Now Saturdays !!

I want to go into business, but I don't have the money. Find the resources and **Start Now**!!

I want to workout, but I need a trainer. Walk, jog, jump rope, do push-ups, do crunches, watch YouTube videos, and Start Now!!

I don't think I'm smart enough to finish school. Study, get a tutor, get around people that have already passed and ask questions You are a genius. All you have to do is Start Now!!

> "IF YOU CAN'T FLY, THEN RUN. IF YOU CAN'T RUN, THEN WALK. IF YOU CAN"T WALK, THEN CRAWL, BUT WHATEVER YOU DO, YOU HAVE YO KEEP MOVING FORWARD."
>
> -MLK

IN ORDER TO MOVE FORWARD, YOU MUST START NOW!!

Let's Gooo!!

WITH NO EXCUSES, NO MORE PROCRASTINATING, NO MORE FEAR, THESE ARE THE THINGS I WILL START NOW:

Keith Davis & Ty Hughey

64

DAY 28: Successful Sundays!!

Whatever you want in life you can have; all you have to do is figure out what being **Successful** means to you and go after it!!

Never mind the bad decisions, learn from the mistakes and move on. No more pointing the finger. Take ownership of your life, your future and do whatever it takes to become Successful!!

> ➢ You can be Successful at controlling your anger which will open up opportunities...

> ➢ You can be Successful at managing your time which will allow you to do more with your day, ultimately leading to more success...

> ➢ You can be Successful at not swearing today...

> ➢ You can be Successful at saving money...

Small victories turn into huge Successful moments!!!

Take the road that leads to a Successful future and Let's Gooo!!

WHAT DOES BEING SUCCESSFUL MEAN TO YOU?

_____

_____

_____

_____

_____

_____

_____

_____

_____

_____

_____

_____

_____

_____

_____

_____

_____

_____

_____

_____

_____

_____

_____

_____

Week Four Reflections

WEEKLY REFLECTION AND CORRECTION:

- ## WHAT DID YOU LEARN FROM YOUR FAILURES?

_____

_____

_____

_____

_____

_____

_____

_____

_____

- # WHAT DID YOU LEARN FROM YOUR SUCCESSES?

_____

_____

_____

_____

_____

_____

_____

_____

_____

_____

Keith Davis & Ty Hughey

- ## HOW DO YOU FEEL ABOUT YOUR OBSERVATIONS?

_____

_____

_____

_____

_____

_____

_____

_____

_____

_____

Let's Gooo!!

Let's Gooo!!

Let's Gooo!!

Let's Gooo BABY!!

CONGRATULATIONS!! !! !!

With completing 4 WEEKS TO A NEW FOREVER, you took control over your mindset. You tapped into a resource that will be with you for the rest of your life!! By taking the necessary steps to become the best YOU possible, you guaranteed yourself success in anything you set out to do.

Whatever challenges that may occur, you are prepared to take them on without a doubt that you'll come out victorious!!

➢ Always believe in yourself!!

➢ Continue to conquer your goals!!

➢ Remember that you are Amazing!!

LET'S GOOO!!

ABOUT THE AUTHORS

Keith Davis and Ty Hughey are dedicated to changing the lives of others, for the better. Through speaking engagements, Teen Summits, workshops, counseling, mentoring, and in a number of other capacities, they have made a difference in so many lives. They will not stop until they help as many people as humanly possible!!

Keith Davis & Ty Hughey

Made in the USA
Middletown, DE
01 September 2023

37629061R10046